A Warm Welcome

A Warm Welcome

2013 Seabeck Haiku Getaway Anthology

Michael Dylan Welch *and* Angela Terry, *editors*

Annette Makino, *illustrations*

HAIKU NORTHWEST / VANDINA PRESS

Haiku Northwest
Vandina Press

Bellevue, Washington

ISBN 978-1-887381-28-4

Copyright © 2015 by Haiku Northwest

All rights revert to the authors upon publication in this book. No part of this book may be used or reproduced in any manner whatsoever without written permission from the contributor except in the case of brief quotations in reviews.

This collection of poems commemorates Haiku Northwest's sixth annual Seabeck Haiku Getaway, October 10–13, 2013, at the Seabeck Conference Center in Seabeck, Washington.

Layout and design by Michael Dylan Welch.

Poems and prose set in 13/16 Nyala.
Headings set in 18/22 Lithos Pro Black.

www.haikunorthwest.org

Contents

Dedication 7
A Warm Welcome 9

Welcome 11
Labyrinth 25
Autumn 33
Cemetery 45

Kukai Winners 53
What Happens at Seabeck 61

Contributing Poets 67

Dedication

*To Jay Gelzer
for sharing her haiku soul*

A Warm Welcome

> "Each day holds a surprise. But only if we expect it can we see, hear, or feel it when it comes to us. Let's not be afraid to receive each day's surprise, whether it comes to us as sorrow or as joy. It will open a new place in our hearts, a place where we can welcome new friends and celebrate more fully our shared humanity."
> —Henri Nouwen

THERE'S SOMETHING ABOUT SEABECK. Maybe it's the autumn foliage, or the hospitality and warmth of our retreat center, but more likely it's the camaraderie of seeing friends and making new ones each year. We welcome many beautiful surprises at our Haiku Northwest retreat, an annual tradition that we call the Seabeck Haiku Getaway. And a getaway it is, too—a release from our day-to-day worries, a time to renew our spirits in nature, and a time for renewal with each other. It's also a time when we gather to learn more about haiku poetry, shared through a long weekend of readings, presentations, workshops, and more. For us, as Goethe once said, "Beauty is everywhere a welcome guest."

Our featured presenter for the 2013 retreat, held October 10–13, was Québec poet Marco Fraticelli, publisher of King's Road Press haiku books and longtime leader in the Haiku Canada organization. One highlight of Marco's visit was his showing of the documentary movie *Celesta Found* (Wildzone Films, 2003), about a woman's diaries he discovered in an abandoned cabin in 1972. These diaries covered the years 1895 to 1916, and Marco had also just published *Drifting* (Catkin Press, 2013), an innovative book of haibun in which he'd written haiku for selected diary entries that told Celesta's remarkable story. A second highlight of the weekend was Marco's dramatic performance of these diary entries and haiku, with Terry Ann Carter playing the part of Celesta.

We've divided the pages that follow into six sections, each with an illustration by Annette Makino. The first four sections are "Welcome" (miscellaneous poems), "Labyrinth" (about the inspiring haiku labyrinth we made together under the direction of Margaret D. McGee), "Autumn" (collecting seasonal poems from the time of our Seabeck visit), and "Cemetery" (celebrating our walk to the historic Seabeck cemetery, led by Alice Frampton). The next two sections feature the winners of our annual kukai competition, in which attendees voted for their favorite haiku, followed by one of several renku written for our "Renkurama" activity, this one titled "What Happens in Seabeck . . . Stays in Seabeck," initiated by Jessica Tremblay (who was also our cartoonist in residence).

We dedicate this anthology to the memory of our beloved Haiku Northwest member Jay Gelzer, who passed away shortly after attending our 2012 retreat, and who we remembered with a brief memorial during our 2013 weekend. In contrast to that sad moment, we also kicked up our heels for our entertaining and often funny Saturday-night talent show. Jay would have loved it.

As Dutch-born theologian Henri Nouwen has reminded us, each day holds a surprise. At Seabeck, those surprises reach us in many ways, through sorrows and joys. Ultimately, that's what the Seabeck Haiku Getaway is all about, to receive each day's surprise with open arms, and to remind us to do so every day throughout the year. Together I think we've all learned to give that surprise—and each other—a warm welcome.

Michael Dylan Welch and Angela Terry

Welcome

open-arm welcome . . .

Seabeck cormorants

dry their wings

Barbara Snow

spinster's estate sale—

a mystery key

among the buttons

    Margaret D. McGee

her cheeks

flushed with desire

snapdragon

    Angela J. Naccarato

midnight breeze—

a weathergram flickers

in the shadows

Jacquie Pearce

western maples

dangle their tassels

the bees swarm

Nancy Dahlberg

haiku reading—

the babel of poets

at intermission

Barbara Snow

late for breakfast—

a new weathergram

hangs from a tree

    kjmunro

tiger lily

the nearness of man

does not bother me

    Jessica Tremblay

claws tangled

in the weft of my glove—

the wren's brown eye

    Connie Hutchison

sixteen buds

on the old tree peony—

we counted twice

David Berger

you have to rise up

before you go forward—

inchworm

Priscilla Van Valkenburgh

butterflies

wasting my time

writing haiku

Marco Fraticelli

surveyors' transit—

my body

measured in impatience

Patty Hardin

empty beach

a set of footprints

out of the sea

Michael L. Evans

so much unseen

in this wonderful world

magic tricks

Angela Terry

over the moon

he asks her to walk

in another woman's shoes

Terry Ann Carter

pruning cedar

their scent

on my fingertips

Marco Fraticelli

the silence

of old growth cedars—

tourists' small talk

Terry Ann Carter

milk bottle caps

the affair

she didn't have

Patty Hardin

dinner bells—

guttural grunts

from the cormorants' roost

Marilyn Sandall

table of mementos

someone asks

the plural of abacus

Richard Tice

first rain

wearing the rings

water makes

Kathabella Wilson

bouquet of catnip I learn to purr

Kathabella Wilson

narrow bridge

do the polliwogs

understand the river?

Dianne Garcia

Seabeck retreat—

no time to rock

in the rocking chairs

Carole MacRury

LABYRINTH

centering my thoughts leaf labyrinth

Deborah P Kolodji

trodden grass

in the labyrinth—

the path we take together

kjmunro

spiral labyrinth . . .
still hoping for a shortcut
to enlightenment

Annette Makino

spiral labyrinth
the sussuration
of footfalls on grass

Connie Hutchison

in the labyrinth

my mind

straightens

    Priscilla Van Valkenburgh

walking in circles

twixt gold brown red leaves

lost   in my own breath

    Susan M. Callan

snail weather

one foot out

of its labyrinth

    Richard Tice

labyrinth . . .

I slow to the pace

of a snail

Carole MacRury

in the silence

of the labyrinth

one clear thought

Susan Constable

leaf light

tree by tree

the path unfolds

Annette Makino

heading home—

a labyrinth

that never ends

    Michael Dylan Welch

conference end

the labyrinth of my mind

unwinding

    Johnny Baranski

Autumn

releasing ducks

one by one

autumn fog

Chandra Bales

speak to me

blue jay

autumn rain

Angela J. Naccarato

deserted lagoon

still holding

the loon's call

Jacquie Pearce

Indian summer

sundogs roam

the clouded sky

Michael L. Evans

geoduck in hand license out of date

Ann Spiers

window gazing

on a crisp autumn day

... the grouch is gone

William Scott Galasso

everyone stops

for this red light

lobster mushroom

Sheila Sondik

constant rain a great mushroom year

Jessica Tremblay

stopping for no reason
suddenly at my foot—
a hedgehog mushroom

David Berger

fir sap mixes

with the wind off the canal

Puget Sound

Carmen Sterba

pussy willow

in a vase of dirty water

the cobwebs

Jim Rodriguez

flashing in the cedars—

finding my bounce

on the bouncing bridge

Vicki McCullough

middle age:

I know the red oak

will surrender to winter's dark

Dianne Garcia

pine grove—

how those yellow birch leaves

capture my attention

Ida Freilinger

night geese—

the leaves turning

in the dark

Michael Dylan Welch

open door . . .

a golden maple leaf

floats in

    Kathleen Tice

a falling leaf

stops short

of the ground

    Jim Rodriguez

fall wind piling leaves
my grandchild sings
the clean-up song

Leslie Rose

a caterpillar's progress
across the fallen leaf
jet lag

Deborah P Kolodji

leaves red and orange my mismatched socks

Johnny Baranski

a few leaves

blow inside

welcome mat

    Michelle Schaefer

last day of autumn

in the firelit doorway

her silhouette

    William Scott Galasso

Cemetery

woodland cemetery

a single spider thread

across my path

Susan Constable

old graveyard . . .

on the gate, in small print

Donations Welcome

Margaret D. McGee

standing at attention

capped mushrooms

beside the veteran's grave

Brenda Larsen

dappled sunlight . . .

coins left

on a child's grave

Angela Terry

a stunted tree

with a few leaves

old cemetery

    Ida Freilinger

beneath witch hazel

her name

no longer etched in stone

    Brenda Larsen

headstones

sunken into the roots

her family tree

Chandra Bales

one hundred years

the age of a child's

headstone

Michelle Schaefer

dead grass

whispering

to the grave markers

Leslie Rose

lately   in the fading purple hydrangeas   sunset

Kathleen Tice

KUKAI WINNERS

First Place (tie)

cracked headstone

coral mushrooms between the letters

of your name

Deborah P Kolodji

inch worm

how do I

begin

Jessica Tremblay

Second Place (tie)

flannel pajamas

my cell phone also

recharging

Annette Makino

neon beetle . . .

her spread wings show

a softer side

Carole MacRury

long grass

the call to practice

doing nothing

Margaret D. McGee

Third Place (tie)

joining friends

   on the porch

      falling leaves

Michael Dylan Welch

June 12, 1893

aged 5 days—

the permanence of silk flowers

Chandra Bales

brittle fall light—

the music of footsteps

on a seashell path

Vicki McCullough

Fourth Place

porch rockers

all empty

after the leaf blower

Richard Tice

Fifth Place (tie)

cathedral in the woods

   all the parishioners

      mushrooms

William Scott Galasso

autumn wind

her wrinkled hand

clutches his

Johnny Baranski

What Happens at Seabeck...
Stays at Seabeck

What Happens at Seabeck...
Stays at Seabeck

Renku initiated by Jessica Tremblay
Guidelines: Write about something you saw,
heard, or did at Seabeck

touching an unknown mushroom

I'm reminded

one day I'll die   *Jessica Tremblay*

silent ceremony

we walk the spiral path   *William Scott Galasso*

every year

at least once

the bouncy bridge   *Kathabela Wilson*

anonymous workshop

who dared criticize Bashō? *Angela Terry*

dozens of haiku

penned by dozens together—

alone *Susan M. Callan*

a circle of friends

sharing another meal *Susan Constable*

eventually

we all arrive—

graveyard gate *Annette Makino*

puzzling over

pennies on a tombstone   *Richard Tice*

Seabeck retreat—

again this year

a bigger circle   *Michael Dylan Welch*

a warmer welcome

at the old inn   *Angela Terry*

Contributing Poets

Bales, Chandra / Albuquerque, New Mexico 35, 50, 57
Baranski, Johnny / Vancouver, Washington. 31, 42, 59
Berger, David / Seattle, Washington. 17, 38
Callan, Susan M. / Bainbridge Island, Washington 29, 64
Carter, Terry Ann / Victoria, British Columbia. 19, 20
Constable, Susan / Nanoose Bay, British Columbia . . . 30, 47, 64
Dahlberg, Nancy / Seattle, Washington 15
Evans, Michael L. / Shelton, Washington 18, 36
Fraticelli, Marco / Pointe Claire, Québec 18, 19
Freilinger, Ida / Bellevue, Washington. 40, 49
Galasso, William Scott / Edmonds, Washington . . . 37, 43, 59, 63
Garcia, Dianne / Seattle, Washington. 21, 40
Hardin, Patty / Long Beach, Washington 18, 20
Hutchison, Connie / Kirkland, Washington 16, 28
kjmunro (Katherine Munro) / Whitehorse, Yukon 16, 27
Kolodji, Deborah P / Temple City, California 27, 42, 55
Larsen, Brenda / Port Coquitlam, British Columbia 48, 49
MacRury, Carole / Point Roberts, Washington 23, 30, 56
Makino, Annette / Arcata, California. 28, 30, 56, 64
McCullough, Vicki / Vancouver, British Columbia 39, 57
McGee, Margaret D. / Port Townsend, Washington . . . 14, 47, 56

Munro, Katherine (kjmunro) / Whitehorse, Yukon 16, 27

Naccarato, Angela J. / Port Coquitlam, British Columbia . . 14, 35

Pearce, Jacqueline / Burnaby, British Columbia 15, 36

Rodriguez, Jim / Washougal, Washington. 39, 41

Rose, Leslie / Shingle Springs, California 42, 50

Sandall, Marilyn / Seattle, Washington. 21

Schaefer, Michelle / Bothell, Washington 43, 50

Snow, Barbara / Eugene, Oregon. 13, 15

Sondik, Sheila / Bellingham, Washington 37

Spiers, Ann / Vashon, Washington. 37

Sterba, Carmen / University Place, Washington 39

Terry, Angela / Lake Forest Park, Washington. 19, 48, 64, 65

Tice, Kathleen / Kent, Washington. 41, 51

Tice, Richard / Kent, Washington. 21, 29, 58, 65

Tremblay, Jessica / Burnaby, British Columbia 16, 38, 55, 63

Van Valkenburgh, Priscilla / Liberty, Utah 17, 29

Welch, Michael Dylan / Sammamish, Washington . . 31, 40, 57, 65

Wilson, Kathabela / Pasadena, California 22, 63

www.ingramcontent.com/pod-product-compliance
Lightning Source LLC
Chambersburg PA
CBHW060218050426
42446CB00013B/3103